More Little Ones

Poems and Songs, 1939
Londoners, 1964
Pleasures of the Flesh, 1966
The Deceptive Grin of the Gravel Porters, 1968
The Gavin Ewart Show, 1971
Be My Guest! 1975
Penguin Modern Poets 25, 1975
(with Zulfikar Ghose and B.S. Johnson)
No Fool Like an Old Fool, 1976
The First Eleven, 1977
Or Where a Young Penguin Lies Screaming, 1978
All My Little Ones, 1978
The Collected Ewart (1933-1980), 1980
The New Ewart (Poems 1980-1982), 1982

MORE LITTLE ONES

Short poems by Gavin Ewart

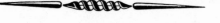

Anvil Press Poetry

Published in 1982
by Anvil Press Poetry Ltd
69 King George Street London SE10 8PX
Distributed by Wildwood House Ltd
ISBN 0 85646 102 4

This book is published with financial assistance from the
Arts Council of Great Britain

Set in 11/14 Palatino by TNR Productions Ltd, London N7
Printed and bound in Great Britain at The Arc and Throstle Press

TO MARGO

In life's rough-and-tumble
you're the crumble on my apple crumble
and the fairy on my Christmas tree!
In life's death-and-duty
you've the beauty of the Beast's own Beauty –
I feel humble as a bumble-bee!

In life's darkening duel
I'm the lighter, you're the lighter fuel –
and the tide that sways my inland sea!
In life's meet-and-muster
you've the lustre of a diamond cluster –
a blockbuster – just a duster, me!

Preface

The poems in this book, like the poems in *All My Little Ones* (its predecessor) should not be read too many at a time. They should be savoured individually, like chocolates. If you scoff the whole box at one go, you'll lose the beauty of them.

Many are sexy – but not, I hope, sexist. A man can be attracted to a woman and at the same time love her as a person. This is a thing that some members of the Women's Movement don't take sufficiently into account.

I am well aware that, to purists, my haikus are not proper haikus in the Japanese sense; nor, of course, are Shakespeare's sonnets proper 'Italian' sonnets. Does it matter?

A proportion of these poems have appeared in the following periodicals, to whom acknowledgements are due: *Ambit, Encounter, London Magazine, New Statesman* (Competition entries), *Quarto, Thames Poetry, The Listener, The London Review of Books, Times Literary Supplement*. Also to the cricket anthology *Summer Days*, edited by Michael Meyer.

CLEARING THE DESK

Just a minute while I throw this badger
out through the window, squash a few squirrels,
blow up a pig, shoot some bloody hawks,
eliminate the bats and tortoises,
crucify all crows,
pulverise a pike, make the owls into omelettes,
dig a grave for the ground-hog!

Now I am ready to write.

A POSSIBLE LINE OF WILLIAM EMPSON

A tie, in dining cars, commands respect

A POSSIBLE LINE OF ALFRED, LORD TENNYSON

The rhododendrons at the end of June

A POSSIBLE LINE OF JOHN CLARE

The little tittlemouse goes twiddling by

SEASONAL TRIPLE HAIKU:
THE TOURIST SEASON

From Santa Croce,
into the warm piazza,
they pour. A blonde asks:

'Where's the bathroom?' She
bugs the Italian guide.
He remains charming.

Another woman
says: 'They sure were a power-
ful bunch of artists!'

AN EXETER RIDDLE

Sitters on the mead-bench,   quaffing among questions,
I saw a thing –   tell me its totality.
A boy sped by,   his feet did not grind gravel,
high was his head,   incautious in the company
of the might of mountains   and a rock-rent liquid.
His hands moved little,   his legs seemed listless,
yet he woke the wind   and exacerbated echoes,
wending not to war   in a charging chariot,
unhelped by horses,   whirling like the wind.
Test-tube technology   covered his completely.
Seen for a second,   he was gone ghostly
as though he had never been.   Vouchsafe me this
                                        vision!

THE DEATH OF A MOTHER

So pitiful and small, such skin-and-bone!

RELIGIONS OF THE ABSURD

What people believe
is often unbelievable.
That a virgin could conceive
is inconceivable!

HAIKU: LOCOMOTOR ATAXIA

Four steps. A long halt.
The old man has a poet's
bad creative block.

THE ATHEIST TYPOGRAPHER IN THEATRELAND

Outside *Jesus Christ Superstar*
it says how it's so long-running
and there's a quote from *The Times*
that calls it 'mind stunning' –
but that's a literal, it seems to me,
the second *n* should be a *t*.

LINES ON THE DEATH OF POPE PAUL VI
BY E.J. THRIBB (17)

So. Farewell then
Pope Paul VI.
My friend Keith
is learning Italian.
He says VI stands for
Veterano Intrepido.

But at least
you weren't called
Sixtus the Fifth.
In the old days
Popes were confusing.

Keith's Mum
says you were holy.
She says holy men
are very good and make
pronouncements
about things of importance
to women, e.g. birth control.

Some said you
were infallible.

Personally
I find it hard to say
what I feel about you.
Keith says
750 million Catholics
can't be wrong.

THE MISSISSIPPI

I am Old Man Mississippi,
full of Time and Mud –
you all must be pretty nippy
if I ever flood!
Swim in me? You would be dippy!
Foolish flesh and blood
would end woeful, dead and drippy!
Keep your distance, bud!

SEAMUS HEANEY

He's very popular among his mates.
I think I'm Auden. He thinks he's Yeats.

THE CRIMINAL CODE

Just one God, right? For me and you
it's God next door, the mate of Stew.
Football we know, we've been to Craven
Cottage – but what's an 'image' and what's 'graven'?
We swear all right, in court and out –
there'd be no fucking life without.
Church? What a hole, like in the head!
All *we* want from a church is lead.
Honouring parents? Likely lads
think nothing's squarer than their Dads.
Don't kill on jobs – unless it's plain
they'd recognise your lot again.
You're joking, surely? Thought you knew,
kids can commit adultery too.
Write it on walls: THOU SHALT NOT SQUEAL
(for us there's no such word as 'steal')
but if free pardons come your way,
then perjure, shop your mates, O.K.?

Don't know what 'covet' is. A man
must grab as much loot as he can.

NORTH LOVE

I never sycamores so sweet
as to behold the walls of York
and to patrol her dimpled feet
as lazy of the minster talk

so happy of the hard-won stone
her weight inevitable bears
a pinkness that is mine alone
and worshipping her tender ears

the lightness of a summer dress
I love some colour of her eyes
the more of me and she no less
whose beauty comes as no surprise

exacerbate the fingered hand
unspeakable the quiet hips
of love such charm as contraband
and not compared the shapely lips.

MOCK CHRISTMAS CAROL

Jesus Christ was born to-day!
Hooray, hooray, hooray, hooray!
Whatever any of you may say
He was born to cancel our terrible sins
And save us all from loony bins!
Hooray, hooray, hooray!

Jesus Christ was born to-day!
Hooray, hooray, hooray, hooray!
This is no time to watch and pray,
Let's all get drunk and drink a toast
To the Virgin Mary and the Holy Ghost!
Hooray, hooray, hooray!

Jesus Christ was born to-day!
Hooray, hooray, hooray, hooray!
Over-eating's a lovely way
To do Him honour; each Yuletide gift
Gives Him a God Almighty lift!
Hooray, hooray, hooray!

HAIKU: THE WIT AND WISDOM
OF CYRIL CONNOLLY

Connolly called the
British 'sheep with a nasty
side'. How very true!

A TITLED LADY

At once a picture comes into my mind of a stately
beauty, topless perhaps, being manoeuvred into a
                                                    ballroom
by a burly footman. He walks slowly backwards,
                                                    firmly
grasping one of her excited nipples in each white-
                                                gloved hand.

HISTORY

Ensuing events impede the backward view.

CRICKET, LOVELY CRICKET!

It's an experimental congruence!
It's a probationary similarity!
It's a proving lucifer!
It's an investigatory rapport!
It's a probing likeness!
It's a dry-run flamethrower!
It's a try-out igniter!
It's a fact-finding similitude!
It's a researchful correspondence!
It's a trial contest!
It's a Test Match!

VARIATION ON A THEME OF WILLIAM BLAKE: AMBITIONS OF YOUNG WOMEN

Some girls long to influence men's hearts
but others concentrate on other
equally private parts.

ON READING THE POEMS OF MATTHEW PRIOR
TO AN AUDIENCE OF ONE
AT THE POETRY SOCIETY

It was one of a series called *Celebrations.*
One Scotsman, a teetotaller, turned up.

I felt sorry for Prior, an admired poet in his day,
and in my opinion as good as Dryden (much
                                        funnier).

I read for an hour, sipping whisky and water.
Afterwards I took the audience to a pub, he drank
                                        lemonade.

Was this a reflection on my reading or the Philistines
                                        of London?
I prefer to think Prior was far too good for them.

DAISY ASHFORD
(born 1881. *The Young Visiters* written 1890, published 1919)

Lords worshipped like the Deity
by the laity!
They must have thought Rothermere
was rather mere.
They had such innocence!
The inner sense
of nine-year-old simplicity
had authenticity,
each well-got-up dainty feeder knew
what Ouida knew:
you only looked quite the thing
if a Duke gave you a ring.

HAIKU: WOMEN IN WARTIME

Every small arms
instructor knew they had a
cut-away portion.

ROBERT GRAVES

A remarkable poet is Graves –
he throws out far more than he saves!
Each time he's Collected
huge chunks are rejected!
Yes, it's true – that's the way *he* behaves!

SELF-ADULATION

There's a foul smell, like pilchards left untinned,
where Rowse, the Cornish Shakespeare, breaks his
                                        wind.

IN A LONDON BOOKSHOP

There's a Scots poet called Dunbar —
they looked at me as from afar —
he wrote love poems, and divine,
a master of the lovely line —
they looked askance, they looked as though
they didn't really want to know —
he knew the Court, the field, the meadow,
'Twa Mariit Wemen and the Wedo',
satires and dirges, never loth,
he used his genius on them both —
they pursed their lips in noble scorn —
among the finest ever born,
he was by far superior to
the poets sold in stacks by you —
they spoke as proud as pigs in bran:
We've never 'eard of such a man.

IN THE LAND OF VOWEL-REVERSED RHYMING

Now strippers everywhere flaunt their white loins
in King's Arms, Dukes and Bulls and the White Lions –
full in the face, to Puritans, vitriol
but welcome to the tillers of the soil
(Scots granite to the Western clay, lias),
who love to watch them wriggle on the dais.
From mountain crofts and flat alluvial plains,
the Dais and Hodges, Micks and Joes and Ians,
combine with Rams, Aquarians and Leos
to worship birds and bushes, tits and toes.

MOZART

Mozart
had all the skill that denotes Art –
his scores totalled milliards
when he was playing billiards.

NOT WAVELL BUT BROWNING

Nobody read him, the poor sod,
He was always moaning:
I am much more way out than you think
And not Wavell but Browning.

Poor chap, he always loved Larkin
And now he's dead,
The critics were too cold for him, his art gave way
They said.

Oh, no no no, they were too cold always
(He still never stopped moaning)
I was obscene and avant-garde and obscure
And not Wavell but Browning.

Note
Wavell was the British general of the Second World War who
edited a conservative anthology of English verse called *Other
Men's Flowers*. To the Victorians, Browning was the last word
in newness and incomprehensibility

A VICTORIAN QUESTION

How could those crinolined ladies
flounce down on pisspots?

NORTH AMERICAN HAIKU

Hail, tribes of Outer
Alcoholia – the Rednose
and Goutfoot Indians!

BROKEN-RHYTHM HAIKU

Our cat
is the greatest thing on four legs
since Fred Astaire and Ginger Rogers.

AUSTRALIAN NOTE

It's not well known in leafy Pymble
that Malory called Pontremoli Point Tremble.

RESURRECTION

On the Last Day the wrecks will surface all over the
                                                    sea.

AT THE VILLA ROSE

The black shit of Hélène Vauquier.

FREE FOR ALL

In a Competition poem I read:
'If I am not a poet
why does my heart bleed?'
And I think to myself 'Quite!
Nobody ever seems to imagine
that a poet's a person who can actually *write*.'

ORGASMS OF THE LOWER CLASSES

And when they come they shout out loud
      'O Didcot!' and 'O Stroud!'
Or even cry 'O Mum!' 'O Dad!',
      'Wowee!' or 'What a lad!'
But ladies murmur 'What a pleasure!
I'm truly grateful, beyond measure!'

A POSSIBLE LINE OF MARY WILSON
IN EARLY 1979

Oh, dear old Betjeman, please do not die!

MUSICAL ECHOES

Who could make, out of musical notes floating
like sunbeams and motes, art?

Mozart.

Which composer of the British nation was
most unlikely to call a station *el gare?*

Elgar.

Who, if a girl in the gardens of Spain said
Play that again! might defy her?

De Falla.

Who wrote a *Bolero* with a theme that a fool
in a dream could unravel?

Ravel.

Whose huge family tree (what a lark!) was
all musical, branch, twig and bark?

Bach.

Who sometimes woke in the night with a scream,
it would seem, crying: *Marguerite is NOT all
sticky with sentimentality and covered in
goo! No!*

Gounod.

A POSSIBLE LINE OF KIPLING,
CONCERNING GEORGE MACBETH

He's a gentleman of Scotland, living South

AMBITION

I tell you frankly
I want to write a poem that is so moving
that it leaves all other poems standing.

I want the readers
to be queueing up like mourners when a Pope dies,
crying their eyes out, loving their emotion,

I want the actors
to dramatise it all over the BBC,
misprints and all, in love and sorrow,

I want it to be
a statutory legend in its lifetime,
built to outstare the twittering birdlike critics.

RURAL RHYMES

I know that God made badgers all
And blessed each hawthorn by the way.
Each animal, however small,
Is there to teach us how to pray,
And every little hedgerow flower
Bears silent witness to His power.

There is a blessing in the rain,
As it descends on me and you,
And in the ripening of the grain
We all can see God's purpose too –
Ah! no escape! We flee, we run,
But He shines o'er us like the sun!

PART OF A LEGEND

Sir Launchalot sails his small pinnace on the Lake of
Love.

CHILDREN'S BOOKS

When you read a line like:
They all took a Day Return to Pigglepopkin
you know you're reading a children's book.
Without funny names children's books could not
exist.

'13 DIE AS COPTER DITCHES IN THE SEA'

13 die as copter ditches in the sea –
    and all the rhythm's broken.
This is the death of our technology –
13 die as copter ditches in the sea,
the printing presses whirr a threnody,
    technical details. No last word was spoken.
13 die as copter ditches in the sea,
    and all the rhythm's broken.

MARTIAL ARTS

1. *Good*

Avidus, greedy for praise, is a good fellow,
he's good at drinking with the reviewers –
no wonder they call his poetry good too!

2. *A Name*

That nobody Shaxberd, whose name nobody seemed
                                        able to spell
and who lived almost unknown in his lifetime,
has done an infinite amount of harm.

By giving hope to so many thousands of bad
                                        neglected poets.

3. *Virago*

Agrippinilla lives in California.
She's well into Cunt Positive
and proud of her bullet-shaped clitoris.

TRIOLET: BUYING RECORDS IN JULY

I've purchased *The Ring*,
I shall play it this winter,

a long-drawn-out thing,
I've purchased *The Ring*

where for hours they all sing,
it's not cryptic like Pinter.

I've purchased *The Ring*.
I shall play it this winter.

BILLY BUDD

The sailorboys all gave a cheer
for their Captain, that old 'Starry' Vere –
he was the bugger
in charge of the lugger
and incontrovertibly queer.

TRIOLET: WINE IN OLD AGE

The old men ballet round the loo
and rise, in turn, from drinking wine.

This is a thing they have to do.
The old men ballet round the loo.

It's like a dance, it's like a queue.
Though bladders weaken, they feel fine.

The old men ballet round the loo
and rise, in turn, from drinking wine.

ALCOHOL

Oh, so slowly the brain starts to go
as the cells are burned out, row by row,
and they're never replaced –
so we're certainly faced
with oblivion – the last thing we know!

TOURIST TRAFFIC

If you're in the market for fucks or
a girl or a boy who just sucks or
desire an Egyptian
of any description –
get going on a slow boat to Luxor.

D.T.

Dylan Thomas was rotund
and orotund
with the voice of a portwine parson.

CHORUS OF A KIPLING-STYLE POEM
ABOUT TEENAGE VIOLENCE TO PARENTS

So it's
     a strong straight left for the Mum you love
and a hefty kick for her arthritic hip!
     It's the iron hand in the iron glove
and some knives of different sizes to give Dad some
                         nice surprises
and the black eye and the swollen lip!

DER HÖLLE RACHE KOCHT IN MEINEM HERZEN!

(Hell's revenge is cooking in my heart!)
– *Die Zauberflöte* (Schikaneder/Mozart)

The Grigsons are a team. They do very well.
Jane does the cooking. Geoffrey gives us hell.

THE HIGHBROW HANGOVER

Today I am feeling subfusc
and as brittle and brusque as a rusk,
most frighteningly friable –
no action is viable –
not a man nor a mouse but a husk!

FOOD FOR THOUGHT

Munchester! Stockpot!
In a train you can eat England!

ANCIENT WISDOM

The Myths are there for micky-taking.
The High Streets are there for money-making.

The Wars are there for killing people,
Old Age to make the strong ones feeble.

Sex is there to bring on babies
and give gay dogs the barking rabies.

Life is there to irritate us
and make us feel our lack of status.

DOUBLE HAIKU: SEXISM

All the tall thin gay
solicitors tell their boy
friends how women are,

without exception,
about three feet tall at most,
with big smelly cunts.

A VERY WISE REMARK
MADE BY HARRY COLLIER
AT CAMBRIDGE UNIVERSITY IN 1935

Why does a publican have a large belly
and his wife an enormous bust?
There's a reason, my acute friend said.
They fit like jigsaw pieces in that *mêlée*
occasioned by conjugal lust,
when they're locked together in bed!

SAUCE FOR THE GOOSE

To hate being a sex object? All very well and good –
and perhaps some men's desires are a bit mean and
                                              shoddy.
But when has anyone been thrown out of the
                                              sisterhood
for lusting after another woman's body?

44

VIOLENT PASSIONS

The mouth can be quite nasty in a bite
The lover's pinch can be malicious too
Legs kick, as well as tangle, in a bed

Words can be harsh and not console or rhyme
Fighting is also love's especial food
Hands can enlace with hands or round a neck

The tools that pierce can be unyielding steel
Attractive nails can score, like claws, the face
Fingers can spread on cheeks, harmful and strong

Hair can be pulled in war, that's stroked in peace
The fighting female differs from the male
The spitting cat attacks the barking dog

WHO IS CIRCE?

Who is Circe? what is she,
That all these swine commend her?
Sexy, bald, and drunk is she;
The Devil such force did lend her.
Underneath the Upas Tree
All the fiends attend her.

WELTANSCHAUUNG

If you look at the world, it looks bad!
And this can make some people sad.
The slightly demented
are fairly contented,
the happiest ones are quite mad.

THE YOUNG POET IN THE LITERARY WORLD

The big insensitive faces / come up to you at parties
and you are wondering
who that terrible-looking fat tart is,

and she turns out to be a / greatly revered novelist
and that old purple man
a Prize-Winning Poet – unless you're pissed.

The words may have been winning / but the flesh is
                                                            weak;
like everyone's, it ages.
A profile like that of an Ancient Greek

is foxed so much more quickly / than the humble
                                                            paper
that holds a masterpiece –
grave marks stain hands, all that kind of caper.

You think they should look noble? / but no it doesn't
                                                            follow.
Each is just the mould that
once formed the statue; and, like all moulds, they're
                                                            hollow.

DIVORCED WOMEN IN DORMITORY TOWNS

The lives they travel in are like comfortable cars –
but they bore them. Oh, nothing happens!
With enough money and custody of the children,
do they sometimes regret the drunken husbands?

Lovers are hard to come by. Romance
in the brash shapes of feminine longing
left them twenty years ago. All that equipment
simply languishes unused in houses with gardens.

They are most like the day-trippers who drive
into safari parks. They're afraid to go out
into the world of lions. Claustrophobes,
they watch their sweet bodies shrivel like grapes.

MARTIAL AND DOMITIAN

('The Book Of The Games')

In those days it wasn't keeping up with the Joneses —
it was keeping in with the Emperors.

If he held Games, you had to praise them.
After all, look what he provided!
The amphitheatre filled with water, for a real sea
                                        battle,
women killing lions on the dry sand,
a condemned criminal crucified *and* eaten by animals,
tigresses fighting lions, bears elephants,
a rhinoceros goring a bull like an old leather ball —
a genuine banquet of assorted cruelties.

How could anyone fail to praise an Emperor like
                                        that?

A LINE THAT MIGHT BE A STUMBLING BLOCK TO THE PURITAN FAITHFUL

The patriarchs, with all their concubines

HAIKU: MRS X

An old police dog
sniffs my knickers. I charge him
£8,000. Wow!

HAIKU: THIRTY YEARS AGO

I climbed up her white
redbushed body. She had big
green eyes like a cat's.

HAIKU: FOREPLAY

Undressing, she laugh-
ingly hung her panties on
his hard hatrack cock.

50

REPUTATIONS

Poets are very touchy. They have to be the greatest.
Or (if not quite *that*) at least the latest.

A HAIR OF THE DOGGEREL

It's so unfair that alcohol makes you fat
and feel, next day, like a half-dead bat.
The Devil's at the bottom of this, it's understood, for

                                                           you

would expect something so nice
to be terribly good for you.

THE SAD WIDOW

Candy-floss Blackpool, wet and windy, with the
                                                sadness
of the sad sad widow
Pier and ballroom, hotel bar window, with the
                                                sadness
of the sad sad candy
Flossy sea-spray, wrought iron, whelk-smell, with the
                                                sadness
of the sad sad Blackpool
Popping brown seaweed, chip shops, windy, with the
                                                sadness
of the sad sad widow

Blackpool, rock pool, boarders, sandworms, with the
                                                sadness
of the sad sad widow
Thin landladies, thin-sliced bacon, with the sadness
of the sad sad wetness
Sea wind, raincoats, crab claws, windblown, with the
                                                sadness
of the sad sad floss-stick
Ballroom, bar-room, bright lights, rainstorms, with the
                                                sadness
of the sad sad widow

Note
This was written on a course at the Arvon Foundation,
Totleigh Barton, as a poem-game. Two or three students,
improvising, act a short piece on a theme dictated by another
student. Spurred or inspired by this, all present then have 12
minutes in which to write a poem on some aspect of what has
been performed.

IN AUSTRIA

When you drink a *Qualitätswein*
you will never be a loser –
this just means the wine is fine
for the fairly choosy boozer.

When the *Bestattungsunternehmer*
takes the butcher and the baker
he is not a loud proclaimer
but a quiet undertaker.

Brandteigschokoladencremekrapfen –
pronounce it, you will make mistakes!
But nothing terrible will hapfen,
these are simply chocolate cakes!

SPRING SONG

Lovers are rolling over like cats in the sunshine,
allowing their tummies to be tickled,
licking one another,

full of the excitement of finding a new person,
happy in the warm emotion.
The questions come later.

Soon they will discover there are two different
    people
involved in these affairs; quite simply,
spring is never summer.

HAIKU: CULTURE

Ah, wee-wee! The great
French writers: Rubberlegs and
Ballsache and Racing!

PANTOUM: WORSHIP

So much I deify your glorious globes
(and kiss your round re-entrants and your cleft –
the Oriental earrings in your lobes
are all you wear) I touch both right and left

and kiss. Your round re-entrants and your cleft!
On your white skin the blacks of body hair
are all you wear (I touch). Both right and left
I see a Heaven feminine and fair,

on your white skin the blacks of body hair,
where both shine with a single, sexual light.
I see a Heaven feminine and fair
that overwhelms me now – it is so bright

where both shine with a single, sexual light,
the two, the privileged, that make the love!
That overwhelms me. Now, it is so bright –
yet comforting, the finger in the glove,

the two, the privileged, that make the love
(the Oriental earrings in your lobes),
yet comforting (the finger in the glove).
So much I deify your glorious globes!

SEPTEMBER

It's warm and it's wet in September
as the summer burns down to an ember –
but the cold weather comes,
freezing toes, tits and bums,
in the two months that follow December.

MUSHROOM-SHAPED HAIKU:
IN A SEASON OF DESPAIR

We think, as we look
at our children: is this the
last generation?

IN MEMORIAM

Like grim death, we say. A grinning death
gets painted on black leather.

Not for these. Three tourist motorbikes
with right of way on unknown French roads.

One looks back. He wavers
into oncoming traffic.

Notifying. Taking the body home.
Telling the parents.

Not work for twenty-year-olds.
Or seeing it.

Hardest of all, accepting it.
Accepting it.

TRIPLE HAIKU: MEASURE FOR MEASURE

Measure for Measure
has three creepy characters –
Angelo, the Duke,

Isabella. Why
does he abdicate? Simply
to test Angelo?

And why does she *not*
scream *Vows! Virginity!* when
he offers marriage?

BELGRADE

The two big rivers neighbour in the North
The early morning trams are suffering elephants
The sliding doors cremate the airport baggage
The tourist blouse can cost a whole week's pay
The spice is hidden, deeply, in the meat
The plums are resurrected in hard juice
The alphabet rejoices, two-in-one

CHASTITY IN BLOOMSBURY

Virginia was right in a way
to keep Leonard Woolf so at bay –
though she lifted her vest
for her V. Sackville-West,
that was only in amorous play!

A PERSON

She's mean and full of minge-water.

COMPETITION PIECE

There was a young lady of Leicester
whose boyfriends all fondly caressed her.
They squeezed both her boobs
like toothpaste in tubes
and then went ahead and undressed her.

A POSSIBLE LINE OF DR SAMUEL JOHNSON

The Pious Reasoner his Tear withholds.